Pansies are Purple

Philosophies for Life

Debbie Newman

Smile Centre Publishing

Revised Edition
First printing 2000
Second printing 2001

© Debbie Newman 2019

Pansy images by Elaine Gribble
Produced by diypublishing.co.nz

Softcover ISBN 978-0-473-49837-5
Ebook ISBN 978-0-473-49838-2

www.smilepublishing.co.nz
www.facebook.com/pansiesarepurple
pansies@smilepublishing.co.nz

A catalogue record for this book is available from
the National Library of New Zealand

I dedicate this book
to my husband, Larrie Newman, the most amazing
person I have ever met.

Thank you for your undying and unconditional love
always, and for your constant encouragement and
understanding.

Thank you for always believing in me whole-heartedly
and supporting me in all my endeavours, including the
creation of this book.

I couldn't have done this without you.
My gratitude and love for you is eternal.

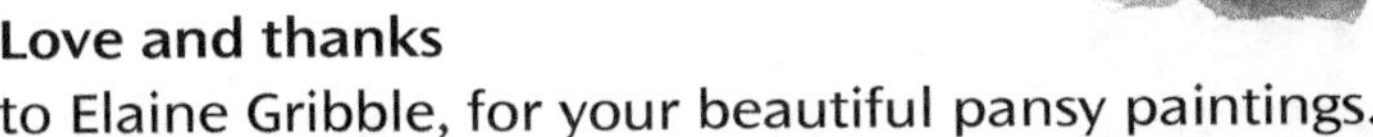

Love and thanks
to Elaine Gribble, for your beautiful pansy paintings.

The true essence of you is reflected in each of them.
Thank you for being such a special part of *Pansies are
Purple*.

May these words
brighten your day
and lighten your load.

May this book support and inspire you
to see life from a new perspective,
with fresh eyes and an open heart.

May *Pansies are Purple* bring
peace of mind, direction, hope and joy.

May you grow in the understanding
that you do deserve love, respect
and acceptance, and that you have every
right to live the life you wish to live.

May you move through life
with a grateful heart.

Blessings,
Debbie Newman

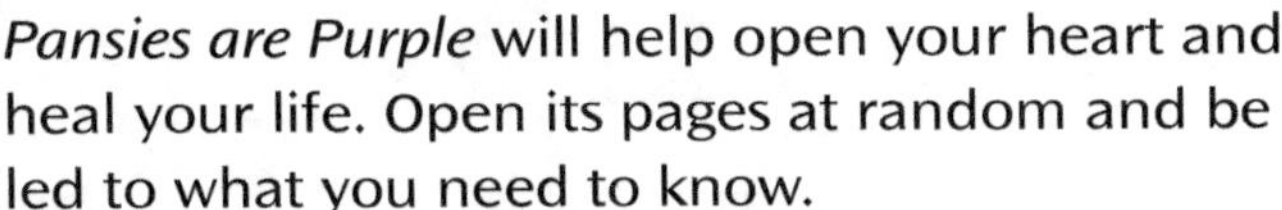

Pansies are Purple will help open your heart and
heal your life. Open its pages at random and be
led to what you need to know.

The left-hand pages in this book have been left
blank for you to journal upon, if you so desire.

MOVING FORWARD

The Athlete

Sometimes on our journey forward we feel ourselves
slipping backward, slipping back into old ways of
doing things, old habits.

This is OK.

At times like this, we are often about to take a
big *leap forward*!

A little like an Olympic athlete, a runner.
There he is on the starting block.
Body lithe, shiny, prepared, expectant.
He has a firm eye on his goal.
He is certain of his direction.

He knows that placing a leg backward
gives him great leverage to bound forward.
Quickly, strongly, deliberately.

He has done his homework, he has trained
extensively before reaching this point.

By extending his leg backward
(symbolically into the past), he is collecting the
tools he has learned from his past training,
enabling him to move forward confidently,
courageously, with belief in himself, prepared.

So, remember, sometimes it is *necessary*
to revisit our past reminding us
of our learnings, so we can yet again
move forward into being more of who we
truly are, with renewed confidence.

COINCIDENCE

There's no such thing as coincidence.

ATTITUDE

Attitude is only everything.

LIFE

A smile is like a boomerang;
what we give out in life, we get back.

SELF-TALK

We immediately think of communication
as being with someone *outside* of ourselves.

In fact, most of our communication is
within ourselves, in the form of our self-talk.
And our self-talk often goes unchecked.

It pays to listen carefully,
as much of our self-talk can be
detrimental to our wellbeing.

Talk to yourself *lovingly*.

Choose loving, supportive, nurturing self-talk
to enhance your wellbeing,
to enhance your life.

LOVE

The more we open our hearts,
the more love we have to *give*.

The more love we *give*,
the more love we are open to *receive*.

SELF-LOVE

Aim to be your 'own best friend'.

MANIFESTING

It is believed we have between
sixty to ninety thousand thoughts per day.

This is astonishing.
We would be lucky at the end of each day to
remember *one hundred*!

This shows how many of our thoughts
we are *not conscious* of.
So, how can we gauge if these thoughts
are negative or positive?
We are unable to.

Therefore, it stands to reason
that the thoughts we *are* conscious of,
need to be positive!

Positive thoughts help to change negative belief
systems; belief systems which have been fed by
our negative *subconscious* thoughts.

Positive thoughts help us manifest
our future positively.

BEING ATTENTIVE

By being attentive
you can often see a connection
between your outer experience
and your inner beliefs.

If you don't like what you
are experiencing in your life,
have the courage to see
what is being reflected for you.

Much can be learnt.

Have the courage to explore
your inner beliefs and make positive change.

Changing your *inner beliefs*
can change your *outer experience.*

GROWTH

When going through difficult times:
Acknowledge
Know
Ask.

Acknowledge …
this is *not* comfortable.

Know …
you do *not* need to be a victim.

Ask …
what am I to learn from this,
so that I may grow
and move on in my life?

SELF-LOVE

We generally think of a relationship
as being with someone
outside of ourselves.

However, the most important
relationship we will *ever* have
is *with* ourselves.

TRUSTING

We don't need to know
how our nose works,
to smell a rose.

CHANGE

As children in a swimming pool
we made a 'whirlpool'
Running round and round,
we moved with the flow of the water.

Then we decided to change direction.

Everyone fought, pushed and
persisted against the flow of the water.

Finally, we began to feel progress;
it was becoming easier and easier.
Before too long we were
running with the current again!

It's like that in life. When we *accept*
that changing direction may include pushing
through some rough water,
we come out the other side a lot quicker.

We step back into the flow of life!

CHOICE

We are never painted into a corner;
we are *always* in a position of choice!

We can always choose how we respond
to *any* given situation in life.

PROCRASTINATION

By not making a decision,
we are indeed making a choice.

We are *choosing* to procrastinate!

SUPPORT

Just trust.

Trust the process of life.
It has always supported us in
what we have needed to learn.

AWARENESS

When we frustratingly ask ourselves:

What am I supposed to do now?
Where do I go to from here?
How am I going to get all this done?

STOP!
Listen quietly.
The answer is there for you.

DESERVING

Let's look at our beliefs
around deservedness.

When pressed for time
and thinking that
we must clean the car,
fold the washing,
wash the dog,
yet are *also* in desperate need
of an hour to *ourselves*,
what we're really saying is that
the car in the driveway,
the clothes in the basket
and the dog
are *more* deserved
of our time than ourselves!

WOW!
Time to prioritise!

There will always
be things to do, places to go.

But sometimes, we need to put
ourselves at the top of the list!

UNCONDITIONAL LOVE

The most important thing in parenting?

Just love them!

ACCEPTANCE

When you're 'moving on' in your life,
never judge others for where *they* are.

They are exactly where they
are *meant* to be right now,
or they simply wouldn't be there.

This is the case for all of us.

UNDERSTANDING

Bet your bottom dollar:

The person who presses your buttons the most,
is the person you have the most to learn from.

INNER WISDOM

A man can travel the world in search,
to return home and find
that what he was looking for
was right under his feet.

The answers were *within* him.

SHARING

For a parent, a child's size
can be deceptive.

Remember:
You have as much
to learn from your child,
as your child has to learn from you.

CREATIVE

When we come to a
‘block wall’ in life, consider:

Is this the right direction,
the right action, the best response?

Or can this be done differently?

ONENESS

A smile is an international
language all of its own.

It crosses all boundaries

It's understood by all.

It is the language of the heart.

NURTURING

We were born
as human *beings*,
not human *doings*.

Take a rest for a while.

There is no person's life
that cannot be enriched
by a smile.

COURAGE

Have the courage
to be who you are.

SINCERITY

Life is really very simple:

Just *love* and *be loved*.

FREEDOM

Have the courage
to 'step out of the square'.

Have the courage
to stand in your integrity
and speak *your* truth,
not the truth of *others'* expectations.

LOVE

Reach out and touch.

The world is in dire need
of a big hug.

EMBRACE

Hug with an open heart
and wide-open arms.

GENTLENESS

Have the courage
to befriend yourself.

PEACE

World peace is not global.

World peace begins
deep within one person.

CONFIDENCE

You truly are beautiful!

Explore that beauty.
Feel that beauty.
Own that beauty.

PURPOSE

Live life with purpose.

Work towards
true unconditional love:
unconditional love for self
and unconditional love for others.

HONESTY

We cannot truly love others
until we truly love ourselves.

DESTINY

When we're on
our *true life's path*,
we feel passionate.

We *do* with passion.

We *deliver* with passion.

Life is our passion.

WISDOM

Listen to your intuition,
your inner knowing.

It is the wisdom of your soul.
It is your soul's truth.

TRUTH

When you ask yourself a question,
listen to the *very* first thing
that comes to mind.

This is usually the *true* answer for you.
It is *your soul's* truth.

We often discard our first thought,
then go on to listen to the next.

This next thought can often be the
left brain 'learned thinking',
derived from our conditioning.

Have the courage to listen to
the very first thought that comes to mind.

RELATIONSHIPS

Everything in life is about relationships.

Be it personal or business,
it all comes down to relationships.

And any relationship, to be successful,
must be win-win.

TRUST

Trust that we are always
in the right place,
at the right time.

TRUST

Put it out there,
and trust that the Universe
will support you.

LETTING GO

Let go and trust the process of life.

See and believe in the vision ahead,
then simply leave the 'hows'
up to the Universe!

PROCESSING

As we go through life,
not dealing with issues as they arise,
it's like stuffing them into a tight cylinder.
The more and more we stuff in,
the greyer and darker it gets,
until eventually, we perceive
life *through* this grey fog.

If we don't begin a process
that starts dealing with our issues,
this grey fog becomes like a pressure cooker.

As the pressure becomes too great,
it shoots from us like a jet of steam;
often expressed with anger,
at an inappropriate time,
and often to the detriment of
the current situation or relationship.

However,
we *can* choose to do things differently.
Instead of stuffing our issues deep within,
choose to deal with them as they arise.

INTEGRITY

Stand in your truth and integrity,
and have the courage to state or take action
on what is important to you.

PARTICIPATE

Become a participator in life,
not a spectator.

LIFE LESSONS

We come into this lifetime with certain
lessons to learn.

With all our little idiosyncrasies, warts and all,
we are perfect for this process.

Know that you do have the ability to meet
the challenges on your pathway.

These are your life lessons.
This is your learning process.

UNIQUE

We cannot compare ourselves
to another human being.

We are unique.

Just as an orange and a banana
are pieces of fruit,
there is absolutely *no* way
an orange could *ever* look like
or be a banana.

TRUST

People often ask:
But *how* can I let go and trust
that the Universe will support me?

Let us consider the magnificence
of the human body for a moment.

Every day there are hundreds of tiny,
intricate systems working
within our body.

We don't even *know* that half of
these systems *exist*, let alone have to think
about switching them on each morning!

Yet it would take only one important system
to break down at some point,
and we'd be 'out like a light'.

Every night when we go to bed,
we just *implicitly* trust that every system
is switched on and will be supporting us
when we wake up!

Now how's *that* for trust?
And that trust is honoured.
So really, anything *outside* of our body
pales by comparison!

BEAUTY

When we were first seen
as a new-born child,
it was with awe.

They said
'Oh what a beautiful child.
What an *absolute miracle*!'

DNA-wise,
we are *still* this same child.
We are actually the same, but taller!

See yourself and others
as just that: *beautiful*.

And yes, *you are still* A MIRACLE.

Pansies are Purple 108 Debbie Newman

If we do not express
our absolute full selves in life,

it's a bit like
being given legs,
and choosing not to walk,

or being given eyes,
and walking through life
with them half-closed.

What a waste!

GUIDANCE

We often go to *the point of pain*
before asking for guidance
from our inner knowing.

This guidance
is *always* available to us.

With this awareness,
we can choose to tap into our inner knowing
and save ourselves a lot of pain!

THANKFULNESS

Be *thankful* for self-doubt.

Self-doubt affords us the opportunity
to explore, heal and grow,
and to find the courage
that resides deep within us.

SELF-AWARENESS

Having self-awareness is important.

When you notice yourself repeating
a negative behavioural pattern,
detach, look at your options,
and ask yourself:

How can I do this differently?

OPPORTUNITY

When one door closes,
another door opens.
This is true.

When looking back on life,
we notice life has been
a little like a 'swing door'.

As one door is closing in our lives,
another is automatically
being opened for us.

Feel safe in this knowledge
as you step forward.

RESPONSIBILTY

Responsibility.
The word conjures up thoughts of
a burden on shoulders.

However, within *responsibility*,
two words are entwined: *ability* and *respond.*

So, the word can also be interpreted as:
having the ability to respond.

Be aware that in any situation in life,
you *are* in a position of choice.

You *can* choose to respond in
many different ways, not just one.

Stand back and look at the possibilities...

Take a look at the flow-on effect
of *all* choices, then make the choice
that feels right for you.

COMMITMENT

When lacking commitment by saying
'I'm going to *try*' to do something,
you're creating room for procrastination.

You either *do* something,
or you do *not* do something!

Your choice.

EMPOWERMENT

Notice when we say the word *should*.

Ask yourself: *Who* said I should?
Often, *should* comes from prior conditioning.

Be honest with yourself:

Is this word *should*
appropriate for you now?
Does it work for you in your life now?

Change the word *should* to *could*.
The word *could* gives you options
and is much more empowering.

Could puts you in a position of choice.

INTUITION

There are many steps
when working with your intuition.

Knowing we *all* possess intuition

Acknowledging you have intuition

Tapping into your intuition

Listening to your intuition

Honouring your intuition

Trusting your intuition

Actioning what your intuition tells you

Live, love, and learn.

OPENING UP

When we've been hurt in life,
it's natural to withdraw and hold back
on the expression of our feelings.

Indeed, the thought of opening up again
to life could feel as vulnerable
as if we found ourselves standing
naked on a football field.

We would immediately
want to cover ourselves up
in order to feel safe.

Unfortunately, sealing ourselves off
from the world works a little like a closed hand.

A closed hand cannot give;
A closed hand cannot receive.

MIRACLES

If there had never been a miracle,
we could never hope for one.

Life is full of little miracles;
we just need to open our eyes to them
and be thankful.

SIMPLICITY

It just is.

What's in the name?

People seem drawn to this book. And I am often asked, why the title *Pansies are Purple*?

The title came from a random comment over a leisurely dinner with friends several years before *Pansies are Purple* was even written. Somehow the name just stuck in my mind, and the book evolved as such. It seemed so right, for reasons unknown at the time. However, it quickly became apparent why this title was apt, why it felt so complete and grounding, why it was destined to sit proudly on bookshelves with its apparently random title.

The title of *Pansies are Purple* (or 'Pansies' as it is fondly referred to by readers) is relevant to the content of the book in many ways.

The true essence of the pansy flower reflects many aspects of the philosophies:

Pansies are a 'tried and true' flower. A salt-of-the-earth flower. A flower loved by multitudes, symbolising simplicity and joy through their beautiful colours, hues and dainty faces painted on their petals.

The philosophies in *Pansies are Purple* are simple, helping to bring clarity, simplicity and joy into the hearts and lives of those who use them. They are indeed 'tried and true', evolving from many years of use within my kinesiology practice.

Pansies are renowned for growing prolifically and self-seeding. They are a mainstay in the garden.

The philosophies in *Pansies are Purple* can be used as personal mainstays, as a grounding influence in our everyday lives. As we learn and grow using the philosophies, the way we respond to situations and people around us changes. We begin to accept the seeds of joy, peace, and unconditional love, and these seeds can often self-seed within those around us. The seeds germinate yet again. Unconditional love *is* a mainstay of life. The prolific growth of unconditional love will help bring about a state of peace in our world.

Pansies are purple. Many years ago, pansies were predominantly purple. Nowadays, pansies are grown in an endless array of different colours and hues.

The philosophies in *Pansies are Purple* are reflective of this, raising awareness that there are many ways of looking at life, and many different ways of responding to life's challenges.

How *Pansies are Purple* came to be

The root of the philosophies

The philosophies in *Pansies are Purple* evolved from my clinic work as a kinesiologist.
My clients embraced the philosophies, regularly utilising them in their daily lives, helping themselves 'keep on track'; giving strength, encouragement, peace of mind, hope and direction.

The seed of an idea

Seeing the progress my clients made by utilising the philosophies sparked the idea of offering them to a much wider audience. I was acutely aware of the limitations in doing so whilst working in a one-on-one clinic situation. And life was busy. The early days of my clinic work coincided with the raising of our three young sons, at times creating some tricky balancing of my time. So, as much as I was passionate about wanting to spread my philosophies further afield, time to even sit and think on how I would do this was in short supply. Consequently, the seed of my idea lay dormant, but I just knew in my heart that it was destined to happen at some point. I knew that when the time was right my seed would germinate. And as it turned out, when germination did occur, I was taken by complete surprise!

Recognising resistance

Aside from my busy lifestyle, another block lay in the way, something that needed to be addressed. I felt resistance to going out into the wider world with my work. It takes courage to stand up and risk standing out. I knew the roots of this resistance lay in my childhood. Having grown up in a small town, I was highlighted for achieving success at a young age. I was thrust into the limelight and felt very exposed and vulnerable. I disliked everyone knowing who I was, where I was, what I was doing and who I was with. I longed for a bit of anonymity. I longed to walk down a street incognito, with no one watching my every move. I think this was one of the factors that influenced my move from my small hometown to a large city at a relatively young age. I revelled in the freedom that city living gave me.

So, fast forward. I gained confidence and became happier in my own skin, but a thread of doubt and shyness still hid within me. Although I believed in myself and recognised what I had to offer to the world, I still hid my light beneath a bushel, not courageous enough to step out into the limelight.

However, as sometimes happens, my mind was made up for me. The issue of '*when* was the right time to publish my book' was taken out of my hands. I had been reluctant to begin the process of publishing, trying to pluck up my courage. I was then challenged by the most profound life experience, which saw me fighting for my life, and ultimately held the power to change my direction and my life. *Pansies are Purple* was ready to evolve.

A surreal experience

On a winter's day in June 2000, I entered a hospital with no idea of the impact this short visit would have on my life. After routine surgery, I was left bleeding internally for twelve hours, with hospital staff unaware of what was happening. I was in a terrible state, with my vitals struggling. When it was finally recognised what was happening, bedlam broke loose. I was hurriedly administered a blood transfusion and prepared for a revisit to the operating theatre and a further three hours of corrective surgery. Amidst all the panic, I seemed to be suddenly catapulted away to someplace else, finding myself in a deep, hollow space of hush, suspended in absolute and exquisite peace, quiet and tranquillity. Feelings of deep love enveloped me, caressed me, permeated me. I seemed completely removed from my hospital bed, totally unaware of the manic happenings within the room.

Reassurance from an angelic realm

Then it happened. Up above, in the corner of the room, appeared two floating figures. Two heavenly, opaque-looking, robe-draped beings, which I interpreted as angels. I initially felt a little startled by their presence, but then came to a rational level of thinking, reconciling in my mind, 'Well, if this is it, that's OK. My boys are all old enough to grow up without me now. They all have a very close and loving relationship with their Dad. They will be OK.' I never thought for a moment about missing them or my dear husband. It was all very matter of fact. However, these thoughts melted away as I was connected to a strong knowing that the angels were there to help me through, that I just needed to trust. I became reassured by their presence; I knew I'd be OK. I felt my inner strength come strongly to the fore. It was such an incredibly profound experience. I was later to find out that this was termed a near-death experience. I don't know how long it lasted, but its impact was immense.

Before I knew it, I was conscious of being amidst all the bedlam in the room again and being wheeled off for my second visit to the operating theatre that day.

Germination occurs

It took me a long time to recuperate, with full recovery taking six months. I came out of hospital with several systems in my body not fully functioning. My experience had effectively placed me in a space of total *being*. I was forced into the role of a human *being* rather than that of a human *doing*. For the first two weeks, I just sat in a chair watching the world go by, very peacefully. It was during this period that the tiny seed of my idea decided to germinate, and I knew with all my heart, it was time. Time to step up and stand out. It was time to put pen to paper and bring my work to fruition in the form of a book of my philosophies.

Pansies are Purple takes on a life of its own

From the moment I accepted that it was time to publish, miracles began happening. I watched in amazement as all doors opened effortlessly, leading the way to *Pansies are Purple* becoming a reality. As unwell as I was, the Universe fully supported me in seeing my project through. My energy picked up and I was pumped with enthusiasm! Whatever was needed came to me: the people, the resources, everything! I almost felt like the process had been taken out of my hands; *Pansies are Purple* seemed to take on a life of its own. It was as if the book was destined to be. It was just waiting for me to catch up, to bring it to life.

An interesting observation: It's as if I had to almost lose

my *own* life in order to give *Pansies are Purple* a life of its own.

Three short months after accepting that it was time to publish my book, I proudly stood at its launching. *Pansies are Purple* had finally come to life!

And just as pansies do, this book has spread its seeds widely; its seeds of joy, peace, love and compassion.

Pansies are Purple has touched and continues to touch the hearts and lives of many.

About the Author

Debbie Newman lives in Auckland, New Zealand. She is a walker, talker, biker, swimmer, singer. She is a spreader of kindness and an avid hugger. She enjoys sharing time with family and friends, and particularly treasures time spent with her fabulous family of happy hubby, three gorgeous boys, their lovely wives and five scrumptious grandkids.

The philosophies in *Pansies are Purple* evolved from Debbie's work as a kinesiologist. Her clients strongly resonated with the philosophies, embracing them and incorporating them into their daily lives. As a result, her clients began leading happier lives, with greater awareness, love, pride, peace, gratitude and joy.

The impact of a near-death experience catapulted Debbie into the world of writing. *Pansies are Purple* had been awaiting its call, and the near-death experience opened the gateway to its existence. Ultimately, the profound experience became the catalyst for Debbie to take her philosophies to the world.

Pansies are Purple is Debbie's first book. However, she intends there to be many more – *Watch this space*!